TABLE OF CONTENTS

Disclaimer	3
About the Author	4
Why Another Cookbook	5
Eat Clean Food	5
Your Clean Grocery List	6
Breakfast Recipes	9
Lunch Recipes	20
Snack Recipes	32
Dinner Recipes	34
Recipes with Five or Fewer Ingredients	46
Thank You	47

Copyright 2015 John Holley All Rights Reserved

DISCLAIMER

The information contained in this guide is for informational purposes and is not to be used to diagnose or treat any medical condition. For diagnosis or treatment of any such condition, consult your own health care provider. The publisher and author are not responsible for any specific conditions which may require medical supervision and are not liable for any damages or negative consequences from any treatment, action or application which may result to any person reading or following information in this book.

It is the reader's responsibility to seek the advice and clearance of a physician before beginning a new diet or course of eating. This is particularly true if you have a history of illness or allergies. The author and publisher of this book shall not be liable or responsible for any illness, allergies or discomfort resulting to any person reading or following the information in this book.

Furthermore, the author of this book is neither a nutritionist nor a dietician and the habits suggested in this book are only guidelines. This is not to be used as a dietary prescription nor should it be relied upon for diagnostic or treatment purposes. Again, this book is for informational purposes only.

Finally, no part of this publication shall be reproduced, transmitted or sold in whole or in part, in any form, without the prior written consent of the author. All copyrights, trademarks and registered trademarks in this guide are the property of their respective owners.

ABOUT THE AUTHOR

John Holley MS, CSCS, PES has worked for over a decade as a personal trainer, boot camp and yoga instructor, corporate wellness leader and clean eating pundit. He brings a passion for teaching others and a sense of humor to his work, which is apparent during his appearances on television, in person and when he writes for numerous online publications. His appearances include those on *Better at Midday* and as the trainer with the *Men's Health* Get Healthy Tour.

He is the author of five books available on his Amazon author page http://amazon.com/author/johnholley. You can follow John's blog http://bemovelive.com, find him on Twitter @bemovelive and like him on Facebook via https://facebook.com/bemovelive.com

Enjoy **CLEAN AND SIMPLE: *Healthy Recipes for Your Busy Life***

WHY ANOTHER COOKBOOK?

You may have chosen ***CLEAN AND SIMPLE*** because clean eating is currently a buzzword like paleo or vegan and the title piqued your interest. Maybe you want to lose weight and need a simple cookbook with easy and healthy recipes. Or you might be reaching out for help because of a weight issue you've struggled with for some time. No matter why you picked up this book, thank you! Just remember, you won't reach your goals unless you…

EAT CLEAN FOOD

First of all, let's agree **you are not your weight**. While the number on the scale is a cultural obsession, its meaning is largely subjective. Your fasting blood sugar, your blood pressure and your triglyceride readings all are more indicative of your health.

Second, **the manner in which you nourish yourself is a reflection of how much you value your health**. Is this too broad a statement? Consider, if you are spending the few minutes it can take to prepare one of the healthy recipes in this book rather than ordering a pizza or getting fries with that, it says good health is important to you. On the other hand, a cabinet full of prepackaged, "convenience" foods reveals you haven't given your well being much thought.

Finally, while our preferred tastes can and do change, **we tend to eat the same foods over and over.** Why not make those habitual choices healthy? The 51 easy, clean and delicious recipes in this book will not only change the way you nourish yourself, but also change the way you think about healthy cooking.

YOUR CLEAN GROCERY LIST

Lean Protein Sources:
Whole, free-range eggs
Chicken breast or tenders
Lean beef or bison 93/7
Extra-lean ground turkey 93/7
Tilapia or Salmon
Tuna in Water

Carbs/Grains:
Oatmeal (Steel-cut if you have time to prepare it)
Organic Brown Rice
Organic Quinoa
Ezekiel Bread or gluten-free bread
Black Beans
Blue corn tortilla chips (no salt added)
Corn tortillas
Brown rice cakes

Healthy Fats:
Almonds
Organic, no-stir peanut butter
Almond butter
Olive oil
Avocado
Cashews
Pumpkin Seeds
Walnuts

Vegetables:
(Any you like: fresh or frozen)
Sweet Potatoes
Asparagus

Green beans
Cucumbers
Celery
Green leafy vegetables
Spaghetti Squash
Zucchini
Spinach
Carrots

Fruits:
(Try to limit fruits to only in the morning or before/after a workout)
Bananas
Blueberries
Apples
Pears
Oranges
Strawberries

Oils:
Coconut oil
Olive oil

Dairy:
(Eat dairy in moderation)
Low-fat Greek Yogurt
Cottage cheese
Low-fat or non-fat milk

Miscellaneous Items:
Organic Salsa
Canned, diced tomatoes or sauce (no salt added or low sodium)
Minced garlic (1 jar lasts a long time)
Protein powder
Unsweetened Almond Milk

Oat Flour
Almond flour
Coconut flour
Liquid Aminos (in place of soy sauce)
Pure vanilla extract
Balsamic and white wine vinegar

Spices and herbs:
(Once you buy them, they last a long time)
Cumin
Turmeric
Chili powder
Sesame seeds
Cinnamon
Parsley
Mrs. Dash seasonings (no salt added)
Paprika
Cayenne
Red pepper flakes
Basil
Bay leaves
Oregano
Rosemary
Sage
Thyme
Ginger
Salt
Pepper

Condiments:
Balsamic vinaigrette
Sirracha
Mustards
Local honey

BREAKFAST RECIPES

GREEK YOGURT STRAWBERRY PARFAIT

Indulge your sweet tooth in a healthy way with this easy breakfast recipe.

Ingredients

- ½ cup Stawberries
- 6 oz container low-fat Greek yogurt
- 2 Tbsp granola cereal

Directions

1 Place yogurt into a small bowl.
2 Cut the strawberries into quarters and place on top of the yogurt.
3 Spoon the granola on top of the strawberries.

Nutritional Facts Per Serving

CALORIES	169
FAT	2 grams
CARBOHYDRATES	32 grams
FIBER	3 grams
PROTEIN	18 grams

PROTEIN-PACKED OATMEAL

Ingredients

- 3/4 cup plain old-fashioned oatmeal
- 1 cup fat-free milk
- 1 Tbsp sliced almonds
- 1/2 tsp powdered ginger
- 1 tsp ground flaxseed
- 1 Tbsp low-fat Greek yogurt

Directions

Prepare the oatmeal before adding the milk, almonds, ginger, honey and flaxseed. Top with the Greek yogurt.

Nutritional Facts Per Serving

CALORIES	420
FAT	9 grams
CARBOHYDRATES	62 grams
FIBER	7 grams
PROTEIN	20 grams

CINNAMON WALNUT OATMEAL

Ingredients

- 3/4 cup plain old-fashioned oatmeal
- 1 cup fat-free milk
- 1 Tbsp chopped walnuts
- 1 tsp cinnamon

Directions

Mix the ingredients in a microwavable bowl and nuke for 2 minutes. Add honey if desired.

Nutritional Facts Per Serving

CALORIES	365
FAT	9 grams
CARBOHYDRATES	62 grams
FIBER	7 grams
PROTEIN	20 grams

BERRY BREAKFAST SMOOTHIE

Wake up to a delicious blend of banana, strawberries, blueberries and peanut butter. This fruit smoothie recipe is a good source of protein and fiber.

Ingredients

- 1 cup frozen unsweetened raspberries
- 3/4 cup chilled unsweetened almond milk
- 1/4 cup frozen pitted unsweetened cherries or raspberries
- 2 tsp finely grated fresh ginger
- 1 tsp ground flaxseed
- 2 tsp fresh lemon juice

Directions

Combine all ingredients in blender, adding lemon juice to taste. Puree until smooth.

Makes 2 Servings

Nutritional Facts Per Serving

CALORIES	112
FAT	2 grams
CARBOHYDRATES	26 grams
FIBER	3 grams
PROTEIN	2 grams

BANANA GINGER SMOOTHIE

This delicious smoothie is perfect for mornings when you don't think you have time for breakfast.

Ingredients

- 1 banana, sliced
- 3/4 cup (6 ounces) Greek yogurt
- 1/2 tsp freshly grated ginger

Directions

In a blender, combine the banana, yogurt and ginger. Blend until smooth.

Recipe Tips
If you're not accustomed to the strength of fresh grated ginger, start with ¼ tsp.

Makes 1 Serving

Nutritional Facts Per Serving

CALORIES	157
FAT	1 gram
CARBOHYDRATES	34 grams
FIBER	2 grams
PROTEIN	5 grams

GREEN TEA, BLUEBERRY, BANANA SMOOTHIE

Ingredients

- 3 Tbsp water
- 1 green tea bag
- 1 1/2 cup frozen blueberries
- 1/2 med banana
- 3/4 cup almond milk

Directions

1 Add one green tea bag to a cup of hot water and steep 3 minutes. Remove the tea bag.
2 Puree berries, banana, and milk in a blender.
3 Add tea to blender. Blend ingredients on ice crush or highest setting until smooth.

Recipe Tips
If stored for several hours in a Thermos, shake vigorously before pouring. The smoothie will be tasty, but thinner than when freshly made.

Makes 1 Serving

Nutritional Facts Per Serving

CALORIES	269
FAT	3 grams
CARBOHYDRATES	63 grams
FIBER	8 grams
PROTEIN	4 grams

SCRAMBLED EGGS WITH SALMON, ASPARAGUS AND GOAT CHEESE

Try it....you will love it. This smoked salmon, asparagus, and goat cheese scramble is full of healthy fats and lots of protein.

Ingredients

- 1 Tbsp butter
- 8 stalks asparagus, woody bottoms removed, chopped into 1" pieces
- salt and black pepper to taste
- 8 eggs
- 1/4 cup crumbled fresh goat cheese
- 4 oz smoked salmon, chopped

Directions

1 Heat the butter in a large nonstick skillet or saute pan over medium heat. When the butter begins to foam, add the asparagus and cook until just tender. Season with salt and pepper to taste.
2 Crack the eggs into a large bowl and whisk with the milk. Season with a few pinches of salt and pepper and add to the pan with the asparagus.
3 Turn the heat down to low and use a wooden spoon to constantly stir and scrape the eggs until they begin to form soft curds. A minute before they're done, stir in the goat cheese.
4 Remove from the heat when the eggs are still creamy and soft (remember, scrambled eggs are like meat-- they continue to cook even after you cut the heat) and fold in the smoked salmon.

Recipe Tips
Don't like asparagus? Try substituting green pepper, zucchini or spinach for a megadose of vitamins and fiber.

Makes 4 Servings

Nutritional Facts Per Serving

CALORIES	328
FAT	20 grams
CARBOHYDRATES	3 grams
FIBER	1 gram
PROTEIN	33 grams

RED PEPPER SCRAMBLE

Including prep and cook time, this scramble will take you only four minutes.

Ingredients

- 3 eggs
- 1/2 cup pre-sliced fresh red bell pepper
- 1 oz feta or goat cheese

Directions

1 Crack and whisk eggs in a bowl.
2 Add red bell pepper and cheese.
3 Add eggs to a warm pan coated with non-stick spray. Cook and scramble until firm.

Makes 1 Serving

Nutritional Facts Per Serving

CALORIES	293
FAT	19 grams
CARBOHYDRATES	3 grams
FIBER	1 gram
PROTEIN	28 grams

TOMATO FETA SCRAMBLE

Ingredients

- 1 Tbsp butter
- 1 medium tomato chopped into 1" pieces
- Salt and black pepper to taste
- 3 eggs
- 1 Tbsp crumbled feta

Directions

1 Heat the butter in a large, nonstick saute pan over medium heat.
2 Crack the eggs into a large bowl and whisk with the milk. Season with a few pinches of salt and pepper. Cook and scramble until firm.
3 A minute before they're done, stir in the feta.
4 Sprinkle tomato over the eggs and enjoy.

Makes 1 Serving

Nutritional Facts Per Serving

CALORIES	310
FAT	20 grams
CARBOHYDRATES	3 grams
FIBER	1 gram
PROTEIN	21 grams

BREAKFAST BURRITOS

Are you craving Mexican food, but not the fat and calories that accompany your favorite dish? These breakfast burritos are the perfect alternative. Use egg whites instead of regular eggs to cut back on fat and cholesterol. Flavor as desired with salsa.

Ingredients

- Vegetable cooking spray
- 2 egg whites
- 2 corn tortillas
- 1/4 cup low-fat cheese
- 1/4 cup rinsed canned beans (such as pinto beans or black beans)
- Salsa (to taste)

Directions

1 Spray vegetable cooking spray into a frying pan.
2 Scramble the egg whites in the pan.
3 Place the cooked eggs on the tortillas.
4 Sprinkle the cheese over the eggs.
5 Place the beans over the cheese and eggs.
6 Roll each tortilla into a wrap and microwave for 30 seconds.
7 Spoon salsa on top.

Recipe Tips

Add your favorite vegetables such as zucchini, spinach and tomatoes to increase the nutritional punch of this recipe.

If you don't like corn tortillas and aren't following a gluten-free diet, substitute whole wheat flour tortillas.

Makes 1 Serving

Nutritional Facts Per Serving

CALORIES	283
FAT	4 grams
CARBOHYDRATE	50 grams
FIBER	7 grams
PROTEIN	23 grams

BLUEBERRY MULTIGRAIN WAFFLES

These multigrain waffles are high in fiber and low in fat. They are perfect for brunch.

Ingredients

- 1 1/2 cups almond flour
- 1/2 cup rolled oats
- 1/2 tsp baking powder
- 1/2 tsp baking soda
- 1/2 tsp salt
- 1 2/3 cups fat-free milk
- 2 egg whites
- 1 Tbsp canola oil
- 2 cups blueberries
- 1 1/2 cups sliced strawberries

Directions

1 Preheat the oven to 200°F. Coat a baking sheet with cooking spray.
2 In a large bowl, combine the flour, oats, baking powder, baking soda, and salt.
3 In a medium bowl, combine the milk, egg whites and oil. Add to the flour mixture and stir until blended. Fold in 1 cup of the blueberries.
4 Coat a nonstick waffle iron with cooking spray and preheat.
5 Pour 1/2 cup of the batter onto the center of the iron and cook for 5 minutes, or until the waffle is golden. Place the waffles on the baking sheet in the oven to keep warm.
6 Repeat with the remaining batter to make a total of 8 waffles.
7 Meanwhile, in a small saucepan over medium heat, combine the remaining 1 cup of blueberries and the strawberries.
8 Cook for 5 minutes, or until the berries are softened and the mixture is hot. Serve with the waffles.

Recipe Tips

This batter also makes excellent pancakes. To make pancakes, measure 2 cups of the dry mix into a bowl and then add the liquid ingredients from the recipe.

Makes 8 Servings

Nutritional Facts Per Serving

CALORIES	222
FAT	3 grams
CARBOHYDRATES	45 grams
FIBER	4 grams
PROTEIN	6 grams

TURKEY, CHEDDAR AND GUACAMOLE SANDWICH

Forget the Egg McMuffin and substitute lean turkey for Canadian bacon, add tomato and crown it all with a spread of heart-healthy guacamole.

Ingredients

- 1 tsp canola or olive oil
- 2 egg whites
- Salt and black pepper to taste
- 2 oz smoked turkey breast
- 1 slice reduced-fat cheese
- 1 thick slice tomato
- 1 Ezekiel brand or gluten-free English muffin, split and toasted
- 1 Tbsp avocado

Directions

1 Heat the oil in a small nonstick saute pan over medium heat. Add the egg whites and gently fry until the white is set, about 5 minutes. Season with salt and pepper.
2 Place the turkey on a plate, top with the cheese, and microwave for 30 to 45 seconds, until the turkey is hot and the cheese is melted.
3 Place the tomato on the bottom half of the English muffin and season with salt and pepper. Top with the turkey and egg. Slather the avocado on the top and enjoy.

Recipe Tips

Smoked meat products can be high in sodium. Look for turkey with fewer than 500 milligrams of sodium per serving.

Makes 1 Serving

Nutritional Facts Per Serving

CALORIES	360
FAT	14 grams
CARBOHYDRATES	34 grams
FIBER	6 grams
PROTEIN	26 grams

LUNCH RECIPES

FETA AND TOMATO SALAD

This is an easy twist on the Caprese Salad.

Ingredients

- 1 medium tomato, cubed
- 1 oz feta cheese
- 1 cup fresh spinach leaves
- 1 clove garlic, pressed
- 1 1/2 tsp olive oil
- 2 Tbsp balsamic vinegar
- 1/4 tsp black pepper

Directions

Combine all ingredients for *1 Serving*

Nutritional Facts Per Serving

CALORIES	242
FAT	16 grams
CARBOHYDRATES	15 grams
FIBER	3 grams
PROTEIN	11 grams

GRILLED CHICKEN SALAD WITH CRANBERRIES, AVOCADO, GOAT CHEESE

In the hands of a restaurant line cook, a harmless bowl of greens turns into a high-calorie mash-up of dressing, cheese and croutons. Make your salad at home and you're guaranteed to cut that number in half.

Ingredients

- 12 oz cooked chicken
- 12 cups arugula (1 prewashed bag)
- 1/4 cup dried cranberries
- 1 avocado, pitted, peeled, and sliced
- 1/4 cup crumbled goat cheese
- 1/4 cup walnuts, roughly chopped
- 1/4 cup Honey Mustard Vinaigrette

Directions

Combine the chicken, arugula, cranberries, avocado, goat cheese, walnuts, vinaigrette, salt and pepper in a large bowl, using 2 forks to incorporate the dressing.

Makes 4 Servings

Nutritional Facts Per Serving

CALORIES	476
FAT	24 grams
CARBOHYDRATES	13 grams
FIBER	4 grams
PROTEIN	53 grams

CHILI-SPICED SALMON SALAD

You'll love this combination of salmon with avocado, grapefruit sections, onions and beets over a bed of Bibb lettuce.

Ingredients

- 4 oz canned or grilled salmon
- 3 cups Bibb lettuce, torn into bite-size pieces
- 1/4 avocado, diced
- 1 pink grapefruit, sectioned
- 2 slices red onion
- 1/2 cup canned beets, drained and diced
- 10 pistachio nuts, shelled and chopped

Dressing

- 2 Tbsp fresh orange juice
- 1 Tbsp extra-virgin olive oil
- 2 tsp white wine vinegar
- 1/2 tsp Dijon mustard
- 1 large pinch kosher salt
- 1 large pinch chili powder

Directions

1 Combine all dressing ingredients in a blender or food processor, or whisk together until smooth.
2 In a large bowl, combine salmon, lettuce, avocado, grapefruit, onion, and beets. Toss well with dressing.
3 Sprinkle with pistachios.

Recipe Tips
Save time in the future when you're making this or other salads, and prepare a double or triple batch of dressing. It goes well on kale, spinach and turnip greens.

Makes 2 Servings

Nutritional facts Per Serving

CALORIES	283
FAT	12 grams
CARBOHYDRATES	25 grams
FIBER	5 grams
PROTEIN	14 grams

SPINACH, GOAT CHEESE AND WALNUT SALAD

This salad is a delicious way to get your spinach and healthy fats.

Ingredients

- 3 cups baby spinach leaves
- 1 Tbsp balsamic vinegar
- 2 Tbsp orange juice
- ½ tsp Dijon mustard
- 2 oz goat cheese
- 1 Tbsp chopped walnuts

Directions

1 Combine vinegar, orange juice, mustard and oil in a small bowl and mix well.
2 Place spinach in serving bowl, drizzle with dressing and toss to blend.
3 Toss spinach mixture with goat cheese, walnuts and fresh vegetables (if desired).

Makes 2 Servings

Nutritional facts Per Serving

CALORIES	317
FAT	22 grams
CARBOHYDRATES	18 grams
FIBER	5 grams
PROTEIN	15 grams

BERRY GOAT CHEESE SALAD

Cook an extra chicken breast at dinner and then toss it with strawberries, blueberries, walnuts, tomatoes, and spinach. If berries are out of season, frozen ones will work, too.

Ingredients

- 1 Tbsp walnuts
- 3 cups baby spinach
- 1/2 cup halved strawberries
- 1/2 cup blueberries
- 1 yellow tomato, cut into eighths
- 2 purple radishes, thinly sliced
- 1 skinless chicken breast (6 oz), grilled
- 1 Tbsp goat cheese crumbles

Dressing

- ¼ cup sliced strawberries
- 1 Tbsp fresh orange juice
- 1 ½ tsp red wine vinegar
- 2 Tbsp nonfat Greek yogurt

Directions

1 Combine all dressing ingredients in a blender or food processor, or whisk together until smooth.
2 Toast the walnuts in a 400°F oven for 2 minutes. Remove from oven. Set aside.
3 In a large bowl, combine spinach, berries, tomato, and radishes. Drizzle with dressing. Toss the ingredients gently.
4 Divide salad between 2 plates. Place half the chicken on top of each salad. Sprinkle with nuts and goat cheese.

Recipe Tips

For an easy and healthy snack, toast extra walnuts and enjoy a small handful once a day.

Makes 2 Servings

Nutritional Facts Per Serving

CALORIES	222
FAT	6 grams
CARBOHYDRATES	21 grams
FIBER	5 grams
PROTEIN	23 grams

GRILLED CHICKEN AND PINEAPPLE SANDWICH

Looking for a not-so-ordinary chicken recipe?

Ingredients

- 4 boneless, skinless chicken breasts (4 to 6 oz each)
- 4 pineapple slices (1/2-inch thick)
- 1/4 cup pickled jalapeno slices, or 1 fresh jalapeno, thinly sliced
- Teriyaki sauce
- 4 slices Swiss cheese
- 4 Ezekiel or gluten-free rolls
- 1/2 medium red onion, thinly sliced

Directions

1 Combine chicken and enough teriyaki sauce to cover it in a re-sealable plastic bag.
2 Marinate in the refrigerator for at least 30 minutes and up to 12 hours.
3 Heat a grill until hot (you shouldn't be able to hold your hand above the grates for more than 5 seconds). Remove chicken from marinade and place on the grill; discard any remaining marinade.
4 Cook for 4 to 5 minutes, flip, and immediately add cheese to each breast. Continue cooking until cheese is melted and chicken is lightly charred and firm to the touch. Remove from grill; set aside.
5 While chicken rests, add pineapple and rolls to the grill. Cook rolls until they're lightly toasted, and pineapple slices until they're soft and caramelized, about 2 minutes per side.
6 Top each roll with chicken, pineapple, red onion, and jalapeno slices. If you like, drizzle chicken with a bit more teriyaki sauce.

Recipe Tips

If you normally don't marinate your meat, you'll enjoy the tender and flavorful result.

If you are watching your sodium intake, use lower sodium teriyaki sauce or marinate the chicken in pineapple juice instead.

Makes 4 Servings

Nutritional Facts Per Serving

CALORIES	387
FAT	13 grams
CARBOHYDRATES	29 grams
FIBER	3 grams
PROTEIN	36 grams

CHICKEN PANINI

For a satisfying lunch, layer sliced chicken breast, black forest ham, and Swiss cheese on a wheat roll and serve with marinara sauce on the side.

Ingredients

- 6 oz sliced low-fat Swiss
- 4 oz sliced reduced-sodium Black Forest deli ham
- 4 oz sliced reduced-sodium deli chicken breast
- 4 Ezekiel or gluten-free rolls (12 oz total), sliced and gutted
- 1/2 C marinara sauce, heated

Directions

1 Heat lightly oiled grill or panini press to medium heat (or use a grill pan).
2 Divide cheese, ham, and chicken evenly among rolls, starting and ending with cheese.
3 Close sandwiches and grill, flipping and pressing them with spatula if necessary, until golden brown on both sides and cheese is melted, about 5 minutes total.
4 Halve sandwiches and serve with marinara sauce for dipping.

Makes 4 Servings

Nutritional Facts Per Serving

CALORIES	292
FAT	6 grams
CARBOHYDRATES	34 grams
FIBER	5 grams
PROTEIN	27 grams

ITALIAN BLT SANDWICH

Upgrade your BLT with arugula, pesto, and turkey bacon.

Ingredients

- 2 tsp refrigerated reduced-fat pesto
- 2 pieces Ezekiel or gluten-free bread
- 1/4 cup arugula or 2 large lettuce leaves
- 1/2 small vine-ripened tomato, sliced
- 3 slices cooked turkey bacon, halved crosswise
- 1 carrot, cut into sticks

Directions

1 Spread the pesto on one side of the bread.
2 Top with the arugula or lettuce, tomato, bacon, and other side of the bread.
3 Cut in half and serve with the carrot sticks.

Makes 2 Servings

Nutritional Facts Per Serving

CALORIES	334
FAT	18 grams
CARBOHYDRATES	29 grams
FIBER	5 grams
PROTEIN	16 grams

TURKEY AND CUCUMBER SANDWICH

Seasoned with horseradish and garlic, this sandwich has a nice bite!

Ingredients

- 1/2 cup nonfat Greek yogurt
- 1 tsp prepared horseradish
- 1/2 tsp garlic powder
- 1/2 tsp ground black pepper
- 2 cups finely chopped cooked turkey breast
- 8 slices Ezekiel or gluten-free bread
- 1 seedless cucumber, very thinly sliced

Directions

1 In a medium bowl, toss together the Greek yogurt, horseradish, garlic powder and pepper. Mix in the turkey and scallions.
2 Divide the mixture among 4 slices of the bread, spreading it to the edges. Overlap the cucumber slices in an even layer over the turkey. Top with the other 4 slices of bread.

Makes 4 Servings

Nutritional Facts Per Serving

CALORIES	275
FAT	3 grams
CARBOHYDRATES	37 grams
FIBER	5 grams
PROTEIN	23 grams

TUNA SALAD SANDWICH

Try this version of a classic, but with fewer calories and more taste.

Ingredients

- Two 2.5 oz foil packs of tuna in water
- 2 Tbsp hummus
- 2 tsp almonds
- 2 Tbsp grated carrots
- 1 tsp lemon juice
- 2 lettuce leaves
- 2 slices Ezekiel or gluten-free bread

Directions

1 Combine tuna, hummus, almonds, carrots and lemon juice in mixing bowl.
2 Spread mixture on bread and top with lettuce.

Makes 1 Serving

Nutritional Facts Per Serving

CALORIES	422
FAT	10 grams
CARBOHYDRATES	51 grams
FIBER	9 grams
PROTEIN	35 grams

ROAST BEEF AND HORSERADISH WRAP

This quick wrap has less than 200 calories!

Ingredients

- 2 tsp nonfat Greek yogurt
- 1/2 tsp prepared horseradish
- 1 Ezekiel tortilla
- 1 large romaine lettuce leaf
- 3 slices lean roast beef
- 1/4 cup chopped tomato

Directions

1 Mix the Greek yogurt and horseradish in a small bowl. Spread the mixture on one side of the tortilla.
2 Place the lettuce leaf in the center of the tortilla, followed by the roast beef and tomato. Fold the outer edges in and then roll.

Makes 1 Serving

Nutritional Facts Per Serving

CALORIES	194
FAT	6 grams
CARBOHYDRATES	24 grams
FIBER	3 grams
PROTEIN	17 grams

CHICKEN GOAT CHEESE QUESADILLAS

Liven up a standard chicken quesadilla with spinach, goat cheese, corn, and cilantro.

Ingredients

- 1 1/2 oz goat cheese, softened to room temperature
- 1/2 tsp virgin olive oil
- 1/4 cup chopped vidalia onion
- 1/2 cup frozen corn kernels, thawed
- 1 pinch ground black pepper
- 1/2 cup diced cooked skinless white meat chicken
- 1 cup spinach
- 1 Tbsp chopped fresh cilantro
- 4 six-inch corn tortillas
- Nonstick cooking spray, preferably olive oil

Directions

1 Combine cheeses in a small bowl. Set aside.
2 Heat olive oil in a medium saute pan over medium-low heat. Add onion and saute for 2 minutes. Add corn and pepper; saute for 1 minute. Add chicken and saute for 1 minute. Remove from heat and, then, stir in cilantro.
3 Divide cheese mixture and spread over 2 tortillas. Layer each tortilla with half the chicken mixture and top with remaining tortillas.
4 Spray a large frying pan or griddle with cooking spray. Warm quesadillas over medium heat for 5 to 6 minutes and flip halfway.

Makes 2 Servings

Nutritional Facts Per Serving

CALORIES	331
FAT	12 grams
CARBOHYDRATES	35 grams
FIBER	4 grams
PROTEIN	22 grams

SNACK RECIPES

Crackers with Almond Butter and Banana

Spread 2 **crisp bread crackers** with 1 tablespoon **almond butter**. Top with 1 sliced small **banana**.

214 calories | 6g fiber | 4g protein | 7g fat

Turkey and Celery Wraps

Wrap 6 **celery sticks** with 3 slices **turkey**. Serve with **whole-grain mustard**.

74 calories | 2g fiber | 8g protein | 2g fat

Banana, Kale, and Almond Milk Smoothie

In a blender, puree 1 medium **banana**, 1 cup chopped **kale**, and 1 cup **almond milk**.

201 calories | 5g fiber | 5g protein | 4g fat

Tropical Yogurt Parfait

Top ½ cup plain **low-fat Greek yogurt** with 1 cut-up **kiwi** and ¼ cup cut-up **mango**. Sprinkle with 1 tablespoon chopped unsalted roasted **walnuts**.

204 calories | 3g fiber | 12g protein | 7g fat

Bagel With Ricotta and Strawberries

Spread ½ toasted whole-wheat "flat" **bagel** with 2 tablespoons fresh **ricotta**. Top with ⅓ cup sliced **strawberries**. Drizzle with 1 teaspoon **honey** or **agave nectar**.

148 calories | 4g fiber | 7g protein | 5g fat

Rice Cake With Almond Butter, Coconut, and Dried Cherries

Spread 1 **rice cake** with 1 tablespoon **almond butter**. Sprinkle with 2 teaspoons toasted, unsweetened, shredded **coconut** and 2 teaspoons **dried cherries**.

177 calories | 2g fiber | 5g protein | 11g fat

Cherry Tomatoes With Goat Cheese

Top 5 halved, large **cherry tomatoes** with 2 tablespoons fresh **goat cheese**. Sprinkle with 2 teaspoons chopped herbs (such as **chives**, **basil**, or **parsley**).

98 calories | 1g fiber | 6g protein | 7g fat

Sesame Popcorn

Toss 4 cups popped **popcorn** with ½ teaspoon toasted **sesame oil** and ½ teaspoon **sesame seeds**.

152 calories | 5g fiber | 4g protein | 4g fat

Mango and Raspberry Smoothie

In a blender, puree ½ cup **coconut water**, ½ cup frozen **mango**, ½ cup frozen **raspberries**, 2 tablespoons **Greek yogurt**, and 1teaspoon **agave nectar** until smooth.

173 calories | 7g fiber | 6g protein | 2g fat

Whole-Grain Bread With Almond Butter and Peaches

Spread 2 teaspoons **almond butter** on 1 slice toasted **whole grain bread**. Top with ½ sliced **peach**.

135 calories | 3g fiber | 6g protein | 7g fat

DINNER RECIPES

CHICKEN VEGETABLE CHILI

This delicious recipe is perfect for your slow cooker.

Ingredients

- 1 lb boneless, skinless chicken breasts
- ¼ cup onions
- 1 cup chopped carrots
- 1 cup cut green beans
- ¼ tsp garlic powder
- 2 Tbsp chili powder
- 1 tsp cumin
- 1 tsp oregano
- 1 tsp salt
- 1 cup zucchini
- 1-15 oz can tomato sauce
- 1-15 oz can diced tomatoes
- ¼ tsp Cayenne pepper (optional)

Directions

1 Place chicken in slow cooker on low heat and add the can of tomato sauce and the can of diced tomatoes.
2 Chop the onions, carrots and green beans and add to the slow cooker.
3 Add the spices, 1 cup of water or low-sodium chicken broth and cook on low for 3-4 hours.

Recipe Tips
Love this recipe? Make a batch of this spice combination and store in a plastic bag so you always have it on hand. You also may want to try it with beef or turkey.

Makes 4 Servings

Nutritional Facts Per Serving

CALORIES	165
FAT	2 grams
CARBOHYDRATES	5 grams
FIBER	2 grams
PROTEIN	25 grams

LEMON HERB CHICKEN

This simple recipe has only seven ingredients, but the lemon adds the tang while the herbs add an exotic, homemade touch.

Ingredients

- 2 Tbsp olive oil
- 1 lb boneless, skinless chicken breasts
- Juice and zest of 1 lemon
- 1/3 C fresh parsley
- 1/3 C fresh mint
- 1/3 C fresh basil
- Salt and pepper

Directions

1 Heat 1 tablespoon olive oil in an ovenproof skillet on high heat. Place the chicken in the skillet and sear for 2 minutes per side.
2 While the chicken cooks, put the remaining 1 tablespoon oil, along with the lemon juice, zest, and herbs, into a blender or food processor and pulse until well mixed.
3 Place the skillet with the chicken in a 400°F oven to roast for 8 minutes.
4 Remove the skillet from the oven and place the chicken on a plate and season with salt and pepper.
5 Add the herb sauce to the skillet and cook on the stovetop for 1 minute, stirring frequently.
6 Pour the sauce over the chicken.

Recipe Tips

This recipe works just as well with a white fish such as tilapia or cod.

Makes 4 Servings

Nutritional Facts Per Serving

CALORIES	155
FAT	9 grams
CARBOHYDRATES	5 grams
FIBER	1 gram
PROTEIN	28 grams

TUSCAN CHICKEN PASTA

This is a meal-in-minutes and it will provide a gradual release of energy.

Ingredients

- 2 oz gluten-free pasta
- 2 chicken breasts, pounded to 1/4" thickness
- Salt and pepper
- 1 tsp olive oil
- 1 clove garlic, crushed
- 1/2 tsp dried rosemary
- 1 cup cannellini beans, rinsed
- 2 Tbsp diced roasted red pepper
- 4 cups baby spinach leaves
- 2 Tbsp grated feta

Directions

1 Cook the pasta according to the package directions.
2 While the pasta is boiling, season the chicken on each side with a pinch of salt and pepper, and sear it in a skillet over medium-high heat for 3 to 4 minutes a side. Remove from the skillet and set aside.
3 Add the oil, garlic, rosemary, beans, red pepper, and spinach to the skillet. Cook, turning frequently, until the spinach wilts (1 to 2 minutes).
4 Slice the chicken and drain the pasta; toss them with the bean mixture.
5 Spoon the pasta into two bowls and top each one with 1 tablespoon of feta.

Recipe Tips
You can substitute goat or parmesan cheese for feta.

Makes 2 Servings

Nutritional Facts Per Serving

CALORIES	405
FAT	6 grams
CARBOHYDRATES	46 grams
FIBER	9 grams
PROTEIN	40 grams

ARROZ CON POLLO

You only need one pan to make this traditional (and healthy) Latin American dish of chicken and rice.

Ingredients

- 1 3/4 cups canned whole tomatoes
- 1 Tbsp olive oil
- 4 boneless, skinless chicken breasts (1 1/2 lb total)
- 1/2 tsp salt
- 1/4 tsp black pepper
- 1 red bell pepper, chopped
- 1/2 cup chopped onion
- 2 cloves garlic, minced
- 1 cup brown rice
- 1 3/4 cups chicken stock
- 1/4 tsp ground turmeric or paprika
- 1 bay leaf
- 1 cup frozen baby peas, thawed
- 1/2 cup chopped fresh basil

Directions

1 Put tomatoes (with juice) in food processor and process until coarsely chopped. Set aside.
2 Heat oil in large heavy frying pan over medium-high heat. Season the chicken with ¼ teaspoon of the salt and 1/8 teaspoon of the black pepper. Brown the chicken breasts.
3 Add bell pepper, onion, and garlic to pan and cook until softened.
5 Add brown rice, stir in stock, chopped tomatoes, turmeric, bay leaf, and remaining ¼ teaspoon salt and 1/8 teaspoon black pepper. Bring to a boil over high heat.
4 Reduce heat to medium-low, cover pan, and simmer 30 minutes.
5 Stir in peas, add the chicken and cook until rice is done. Sprinkle with basil.

Makes 4 Servings

Nutritional Facts Per Serving

CALORIES	471
FAT	10 grams
CARBOHYDRATES	49 grams
FIBER	5 grams
PROTEIN	43 grams

GRILLED FISH TACOS

Make these blackened and spicy mahi-mahi tacos and top them with a mango-avocado salsa for the best fish tacos you've ever eaten.

Ingredients

- 1 mango, peeled, pitted, and cubed
- 1 avocado, peeled, pitted, and cubed
- 1/2 red onion, finely chopped
- Juice of 1 lime, plus wedges for garnish
- Chopped fresh cilantro
- Salt and black pepper
- Canola oil
- 2 large mahi mahi fillets (1 1/2 lb total)
- 1 Tbsp blackening spice
- 8 corn tortillas
- 2 cups finely shredded red cabbage

Directions

1 Mix the mango, avocado, onion, and the juice of 1 lime in a bowl. Season with cilantro, salt, and pepper.
2 Heat the grill or pan until hot. Drizzle a light coating of oil over the fish and rub on the blackening spice. Cook the fish, undisturbed, for 4 minutes on each side.
3 Warm the tortillas on the grill for 1 to 2 minutes or wrap in damp paper towels and microwave for 1 minute until warm and pliable.
4 Break the fish into chunks and divide among the warm tortillas. Top with the cabbage and the mango salsa. Serve with the lime wedges.

Recipe Tips
No ripe mangoes at the supermarket? Both pineapple and peaches would make perfect substitutes.

Makes 4 Servings

Nutritional Facts Per Serving

CALORIES	405
FAT	11 grams
CARBOHYDRATES	42 grams
FIBER	8 grams
PROTEIN	37 grams

SEARED SCALLOPS WITH WHITE BEANS AND SPINACH

Scallops are an awesome source of lean protein, and are ridiculously easy to cook. Combine them with white beans and spinach and you have a delicious dinner in a flash.

Ingredients

- 1/2 red onion, minced
- 1 clove garlic, minced
- 1 1/2 cans white beans (14 oz each), rinsed and drained
- 4 cups baby spinach
- 1 lb large sea scallops
- Salt and black pepper to taste
- 1 Tbsp butter
- Juice of 1 lemon

Directions

1 Heat a medium saucepan over low heat. Saute the onion and garlic 2 to 3 minutes.
2 Add the white beans and spinach and simmer until the spinach is wilted.
3 Add the butter and the scallops to a large pan and sear the scallops for 2 to 3 minutes per side, until caramelized.
4 Before serving, add the lemon juice to the beans and season with salt and pepper.
5 Divide the beans among 4 warm bowls or plates and top with scallops.

Recipe Tips

There are a lot of different types of white beans sold in cans, but cannellini beans are best.

Feel free to add 2 slices of uncured turkey bacon, which for about 18 calories per serving will add flavor to the overall dish.

Makes 4 Servings

Nutritional Facts Per Serving

CALORIES	266
FAT	6 grams
CARBOHYDRATES	25 grams
FIBER	6 grams
PROTEIN	27 grams

GRILLED CHILI-LIME SALMON

This easy and delicious grilled salmon will become one of your favorite recipes.

Ingredients

- 4 salmon fillets, about 6 oz each
- 2 tsp lime juice
- 2 cloves garlic
- ¼ tsp chili powder
- ¼ tsp cumin
- Salt and black pepper to taste
- 4-6 lime wedges

Directions

1 Preheat grill to medium heat, or, if baking in an oven, preheat to 375 degrees.
2 Combine lime juice, garlic, chili powder, cumin, salt and pepper.
3 Spread mixture over fillets and marinate for 10-15 minutes.
4 Place fillets skin down and grill or bake for 18-20 minutes or until the salmon easily flakes.
5 Squeeze fresh lime juice over the fillets before serving.

Makes 4 Servings

Nutritional Facts Per Serving

CALORIES	354
FAT	22 grams
CARBOHYDRATES	0 grams
FIBER	0 grams
PROTEIN	34 grams

MEATLOAF

This twist on traditional meatloaf is low in fat and packed with protein.

Ingredients

- 1 lb lean ground beef or ground turkey (93/7)
- 2 eggs
- 1 cup gluten-free Panko-style bread crumbs
- ½ cup bbq sauce
- 2 cloves garlic
- ½ tsp oregano

Directions

1 Preheat oven to 350 degrees.
2 Combine all ingredients in a bowl, but save ¼ cup of the bbq sauce to spread on top of the meatloaf.
3 Place the mixture in a baking dish and top with the remaining bbq sauce.
4 Bake for one hour.

Makes 5 Servings

Nutritional Facts Per Serving

CALORIES	235
FAT	8 grams
CARBOHYDRATES	11 grams
FIBER	1 gram
PROTEIN	22 grams

CHICKEN PESTO PIZZA

A prebaked pizza shell is the secret to this quick and easy dish. You control the toppings and that makes it healthier than delivery, but just as delicious.

Ingredients

- 1 12" prebaked, gluten-free pizza shell
- 1/3 cup prepared pesto
- 1 cup cooked chicken cut into small strips
- 1 roasted red pepper, cut into small strips
- 1/2 cup water-packed canned artichoke hearts, drained and quartered
- 1/2 cup (2 ounces) crumbled goat cheese

Directions

1 Preheat the oven to 450°F. Place the pizza shell on a baking sheet.
2 Spread the pesto over the crust. Arrange the chicken, pepper strips and artichokes and top with the cheese.
3 Bake for 10 minutes, or until the crust is crisp.

Makes 4 Servings

Nutritional Facts Per Serving

CALORIES	528
FAT	20 grams
CARBOHYDRATES	59 grams
FIBER	5 grams
PROTEIN	30 grams

QUICK PAD THAI

This exotic dish is easy to make with simple ingredients you already have like soy sauce, peanut butter, cilantro, and red pepper flakes.

Ingredients

- 6 oz rice pasta (about 1/3 16 oz box)
- 1/2 lb chicken breast, cut into bite-size pieces (about 1 c precooked)
- 1 Tbsp fish sauce
- 3 eggs
- 1/3 cup chopped cilantro
- 2 tsp olive oil
- 1 Tbsp creamy peanut butter
- 2 Tbsp red chili flakes

Directions

1 Cook pasta according to package directions. Toss with 1 teaspoon olive oil.
2 Heat wok or large skillet over medium-high heat and add remaining olive oil. Add chicken pieces and saute until just browned and no longer pink (about 4 minutes). Remove from pan and set aside.
3 In a small bowl, whisk fish sauce, peanut butter, chili flakes and 1 tablespoon water until smooth. Set aside.
4 Crack eggs into pan and scramble until firm. Add in chicken and cook for another 2 minutes.
5 Add cooked pasta and peanut butter mixture to pan, tossing with chicken and eggs. Add chopped cilantro. Garnish with crushed peanuts, bean sprouts, or lime wedge.

Recipe Tips

Fish sauce is high in sodium, so if you are watching your sodium intake, reduce the amount added to ½ tablespoon or less.

Makes 2 Servings

Nutritional Facts Per Serving

CALORIES	342
FAT	10 grams
CARBOHYDRATES	39 grams
FIBER	5 grams
PROTEIN	25 grams

BEEF AND EGGPLANT TAGINE

This delicious Moroccan dish makes for an interesting meal and it's only 380 calories!

Ingredients

- 12 oz lean ground beef
- 1/2 Tbsp olive oil
- 1 medium eggplant, peeled and cut into 1" cubes
- 2 small yellow squash, cut into quarter rounds
- 4 cloves garlic, smashed
- 1/2 tsp ground cinnamon
- 1 Tbsp slivered fresh ginger
- 1 can (14.5 ounces) diced tomatoes with basil and oregano
- 1/2 cup small pitted black olives, halved
- 1/2 cup canned chickpeas, rinsed and drained
- 1/8 tsp salt
- 3 tsp mild hot sauce
- 2 cups cooked quinoa
- 2 Tbsp chopped pistachios

Directions

1 Heat a large nonstick saucepan or deep skillet coated with cooking spray over medium-high heat. Add the beef and cook, while breaking apart with a spoon.
2 Heat the oil in the same skillet. Add the eggplant and cook for 5 minutes, stirring occasionally. Add the squash, garlic, cinnamon, and ginger. Cook and frequently stir.
3 Add the tomatoes, olives, chickpeas, salt, and beef. Bring to a simmer and cook, covered, for 10 minutes or until the vegetables are tender.
4 Remove from the heat and stir in the hot sauce.
5 Serve with the quinoa and sprinkle with the pistachios.

Recipe Tips

This recipe is a little high in sodium (aim for no more than 600 to 650 milligrams per meal).

Makes 4 Servings

Nutritional Facts Per Serving

CALORIES	380
FAT	12 grams
CARBOHYDRATES	40 grams
FIBER	9 grams
PROTEIN	27 grams

BUTTERNUT SQUASH MACARONI AND CHEESE

A childhood favorite gets a grown up twist in this delicious recipe.

Ingredients

- 8 oz gluten-free rotini
- 1/2 cup fat-free milk
- 6 oz butternut squash
- 1 cup shredded Cheddar cheese
- Salt and pepper to taste
- 1/4 tsp dry mustard
- 1 Tbsp feta cheese, freshly shredded

Directions

1 Prepare the rotini according to package directions.
2 In a medium saucepan, simmer the fat-free milk with the butternut squash.
3 Remove from heat and mix with the shredded reduced-fat Cheddar cheese, salt, dry mustard, and pepper to taste.
4 Pour pasta into 8" x 8" baking dish, stir in cheese mixture, and top with feta.
5 Bake at 375°F for 20 minutes.

Makes 4 Servings

Nutritional Facts Per Serving

CALORIES	304
FAT	6 grams
CARBOHYDRATES	45 grams
FIBER	9 grams
PROTEIN	18 grams

CLEAN RECIPES WITH FIVE OR FEWER INGREDIENTS

SALSA LIME CHICKEN

Combine 1 lb of chicken with a jar of your favorite salsa and cook on low in a slow cooker for 4 hours. Squeeze fresh, lime juice on the chicken when your serve it.

Per 4 oz serving: *190 calories / 1 g fiber / 32 g protein / 4 g fat*

PINEAPPLE CHICKEN

Marinate 4 chicken breasts in the juice of one cored pineapple for one hour. Cut 8 pineapple slices and place on the chicken as you grill or bake it until done. Serve with the remainder of the fresh pineapple.

Per 4 oz serving: *270 calories / 2 g fiber / 33 g protein / 4 g fat*

BBQ CHICKEN

Place 1 lb of chicken and 1 cup of BBQ sauce in a slow cooker on low for 4 hours. Serve with baked sweet potatoes for even more nutrition.

Per 4 oz serving: *250 calories / 1 g fiber / 32 g protein / 4 g fat*

LEMON PEPPER CHICKEN

Marinate 1 lb of chicken in a ¼ cup of lemon juice for one hour. Sprinkle the chicken with salt and pepper and grill or bake until done. Serve the chicken over a bed of romaine lettuce.

Per 4 oz serving: *190 calories / 1 g fiber / 32 g protein / 4 g fat*

GRILLED TILAPIA WITH LIME

Squeeze the juice of one lime over a 4-6 oz piece of tilapia. Grill or bake for 20 minutes and sprinkle with salt and pepper to taste.

Per 4 oz serving: *110 calories / 0 g fiber / 23 g protein / 2 g fat*

THANK YOU

I hope you've enjoyed a variety of recipes from **CLEAN AND SIMPLE: Healthy Recipes for Your Busy Life**, which is my first recipe book. I am privileged to work with many positive, smart and caring people individually, in groups and online. I am inspired by you every day and hope you find joy in your life by caring for yourself.

One of my great passions is to understand and teach the miraculous structure and functions of the human body. I know no matter how long it's been since you've taken care of yourself, it is never too late. I've witnessed clients lose 100 pounds with step-by-step dietary changes and consistent exercise. I've seen people who have smoked most of their lives find a way to quit tobacco and complete marathons. I've worked with people suffering from chronic pain, who dedicate themselves to getting stronger and more flexible and are blessed with pain-free living. I am grateful to have been part of these and many other positive transformations.

I can't thank you enough for entrusting me with the chance to be a part of your life. I am grateful to have worked with many of you in person and look forward to meeting many of you in the future.

Let me know what you think by reviewing this book on Amazon http://amazon.com/author/johnholley, leave a comment on my website www.bemovelive.com or like me on Facebook https://www.facebook.com/bemovelive.

Warm regards,

John Holley

Made in the USA
Lexington, KY
26 January 2016